Offerings

Offerings

Brenda Morgan

'Take only memories.
Leave nothing but footprints.'

— Chief Seattle

Lotus Moon Press

Edited by a remarkable woman.
Cover illustration by Garfield Morgan.
Interior design implemented by Robin Collier.

ISBN: 978-0-9815431-0-9

Lotus Moon Press
P.O. Box 630263
Nacogdoches, Texas
75963

lotusmoonpress@yahoo.com

Printed on recycled paper in
the United States of America.

*To know when you have enough
is to be rich beyond measure.*

- Lao Tzu

Contents

Preface

Transformation is a difficult process tempered by ecstatic joy and dark sorrow. To change our lifestyle we must be willing to surrender the comforts and conveniences we have come to depend on. Elation and optimism will follow success, while failure will be partnered with cynicism and depression.

Our present lifestyle is the result of mindless living for decades. Adaptation is a life commitment. We must be mindfully gentle, patient, and above all, willing to endure.

A mountain is moved
by carrying away small stones.

\- Chinese Proverb

Offerings

In the beginning ...

*My feeling is that we have lost
our sense of place in the world
almost voluntarily.*

- Theodore Roszak

At one time we were all indigenous people and lived interdependently upon and with other species. While there may be some people who still live traditionally, most of us were stripped of our native heritage thousands of years ago.

Civilization occurs when the heart and spirit of those that live interdependently with nature are separated from their ancestral lands. Since we no longer live in the natural world, we cease to understand the world; instead, we rely on those who specialize in taking the world apart.

Over two hundred thousand people lost their lives when the Tsunami struck in December, 2004. The Adaman and Nicobar Islands lay at the epicenter of the earthquake, and scientists predicted that they would be the hardest hit and few would survive. However, these islands are home to six tribes of indigenous people who still live in the natural world and still cultivate relationships with wind, sea and birds. They instinctively knew about the impending danger and fled to higher ground.

If we still lived in the natural world, our interdependence on all that surrounds us would illicit a state of respect and gratitude. But since we live separated from nature, we fail to see the connection between the survival of the planet and the survival of our own species. As a result we never question our investment in the destruction of the world or our investment in destroying one another.

୬

This book is comprised of ideas and thoughts on how we might live more sustainable lives and in better harmony with the earth and other species. We want to understand the relationship between the health of the planet and the diseases we ourselves suffer from; the relationship between our need for resources and how those needs inevitably lead to war.

Offerings

4

Journey

Be the change you want to see in the world.

- Gandhi

I was born and raised in Houston, Texas. However, all of my family on my father's side is from the piney woods of East Texas. My fondest childhood memories took place on my grandparents' farm. It was there that I fell in love with wilderness and the strangeness that arises in those who choose to live within it.

At the age of twenty-two I moved to New York City to pursue a dream in the theater. I lived for ten years in an old tenement building in a disheveled neighborhood, crippled by drug traffic but rich in character and diversity. I performed in some twenty theatrical productions in New York, and then moved to Los Angeles to seek out opportunities in the film industry.

After ten months in LA, I decided that I was not Hollywood material and returned to New York. Shortly after, I received an opportunity to work with a regional theater company in Chicago. I accepted and at the end of two years, I ended my career. It was difficult to imagine spending a lifetime in a profession where women were and are so misrepresented.

I stayed on in Chicago, working as a bartender. One day on my way home aboard the EL Train, I just happened to catch the sunset. As the sky fanned out in shades from burnt sienna to apricot, I realized I had spent the last twelve years of my life walking in the shadows of other buildings, rarely catching a glimpse of the sky; the moon and stars were complete strangers. I dreamed of living someplace beautiful. A whole new chapter of my life unfolded in a rural farming community in the Land of Enchantment, New Mexico.

My small house bordered the Bosque Preserve that stretches alongside the Rio Grande. I was surrounded by the Sandia Mountains, flanked by farmland and apple orchards. My neighbors were coyotes, bull snakes, beavers, roadrunners, great horned owls, sand hill cranes and horses. I went back to school and received my Masters in teaching English as a Second Language. While teaching international students at the university, I pursued another dream: photography.

I was about to expand this dream into a business when I began to have a spiritual crisis of sorts. Here I was, a dedicated environmentalist, and yet every other day, in the darkroom, I generated a couple of gallons of toxic waste disposed of by hazardous waste specialists.

Around about this time, it came to my attention that a teacher, a fellow student, two friends of other friends and a well-known artist had all been treated for ovarian cancer or cancer of the uterus. The only thing they all had in common was they were all photographers, and they all developed their own work. My spiritual conflict came to a close as I let that dream go.

I then ventured into the public schools as a teacher in the gifted program for middle school students. I was blessed to work with students who were African, Iranian, Native American, Hispanic, Arab, Chinese, Philippine, Vietnamese, European, Mormon, Catholic, Atheist, Bahá'í and Muslim. I taught students who belonged to gangs, students who could not read or write, students who cross-dressed and students who were an endless source of creativity and laughter. Six years later I resigned to pursue a different path, that of a writer.

I pulled my teacher retirement, and actively campaigned for Ralph Nader in the 2000 presidential election. I relocated to Northern New Mexico where I

lived in a variety of homes, passive solar, adobe, straw
bale, structures handcrafted from the ground up. I learned
how to use a wood cook stove, chopped firewood and
came to love outhouses as I discovered how to compost
human waste. My neighbors included elk, bobcats, bears,
eagles, mountain lions and tarantulas. I lived without
television and telephones, and began working with the
peace movement.

Peace Action New Mexico responded to 9/11 with
a silent vigil. We stood every Saturday for one hour
through heat, frigid temperatures, windstorms and snow.
It began the weekend before the United States invaded
Afghanistan in October, 2001, and endured through the
spring of 2004. In the fall of 2001, Peace Action New
Mexico sponsored an event with Dr. Helen Caldicott,
Australian physician and international advocate for
nuclear disarmament in the United States. I spoke before
Dr. Caldicott in an effort to mobilize others in the
community to work for peace. This event led to other
speaking engagements, a position on public radio as a
commentary journalist and producer.

When the invasion of Iraq happened, the peace
movement came to a standstill. I treaded in the
shadows of darkness as I wrestled with the privilege
and entitlement of our rich and powerful nation: I lost
faith in movements; I lost faith in political parties; I lost
faith in the congress and senate. I began to see how my
lifestyle contributed to the devastation of the planet and
the deaths of innocent people. The only thing I had any
control over was my own life.

I began crafting a seminar to help me and others
transform our lives. In the summer of 2005 I contracted a

bronchial infection that would persist for three months. I succumbed to the same illness in the spring and summer of 2006. Climate change contributed to extraordinary dry winds in the southwest, and thousands contracted upper respiratory infections. Some developed pneumonia; some died.

Fearing the possibility of long-term damage to my lungs, I left the desert to recuperate at my mother's home in East Texas. There I encountered many people who had similar concerns about the devastating consequences of our lifestyle. I decided to launch my seminar in this small, conservative East Texas town, which led me to Dallas, and as far away as Australia.

Coyote

I stood on the top step, the screen door propped against my shoulder. My gaze wandered away from ancient cottonwoods twisting out of the earth like old dancers to the fallow fields that lay beyond the dirt road.

As I stared into a sun beaten turquoise sky, Coyote loped alongside the fence line. He sprinted away from wild terrain and into territory graphed by barbed wire and wooden posts.

I shouted, "Don't go that way!"

Coyote whipped around, his eyes and nose discerning.

"Somebody will shoot you!"

Coyote stiffened, as he scrutinized the path. He crossed the field to the edge of the apple orchard. Barely visible now, his coat merged with dried brush and the craggy trunks of withering apple trees.

He contemplated crossing the border and then his gaze returned to me. He slunk back to the wild where he would scratch deep into the thicket and sing hair-raising gospel.

Dreams

Do we dare to be ourselves?

- Pablo Casals

I've traveled extensively over the years and it amazes me how often I hear this.

"My cousin, he found the American Dream!"

While the intention to improve one's life is inspiring, the American Dream has far bigger connotations than just better living conditions.

The American Dream for most is making it big in a financial way and then showing the world just how big we made it by parading our possessions. The American lifestyle is our #1 export via film, television, and through the letters and photos of immigrants fostering the dream in their land of origin.

Most developed nations have similar lifestyles to ours, and while their lifestyle may not be as extravagant or as destructive as the American lifestyle, we all need to rethink how we live. The United States has a population of three hundred million people and we consume one third of the world's resources. One child born in the United States has the impact on the environment of three hundred children in an undeveloped nation. Our over consumption and accumulation of goods has put six out of every ten Americans in serious debt. Let us begin by looking at the ingredients that make up our own unique lifestyles.

Fill out the following monthly expense chart to understand your own impact on the environment. Place the monthly cost of each item in the blank provided opposite the item. Use only whole numbers. No one will ever see this chart but you, so be honest.

Monthly Expense Chart

Gasoline _____

Car Payment _____

Public transportation _____

Car maintenance / luxuries /
mechanical enhancement _____

Leisure travel expenses / hunting excursions _____

Insurance (home, auto, life, medical) _____

Mortgage or rent payment _____

House cleaner _____

Gardener / lawn care / herbicide /
pesticide treatments _____

Home repair / remodeling _____

Electricity _____

Natural gas or propane _____

Water / sewage / garbage _____

Phone (land line) _____

Cell phones _____

Storage unit _____

Alarm systems _____

Groceries _____

Childcare _____

Magazines / newspapers / books _____

Cigarettes, chewing tobacco, cigars _____

Alcohol (that you consume at home) _____

Coffee (that you consume in cafes) _____

Videos _____

Cable / Internet services _____

Computer software / games / CD's _____

Sports _____

Entertainment _____

Eating out _____

Spa or gym membership _____

Instructional classes _____

Jewelry / appliances / tools _____

Clothes / sports gear _____

Shoes _____

Hair cut, color, perms _____

Manicures / pedicures /tattoos / massage _____

Cosmetics _____

Pets / livestock (grooming, feeding, boarding, medical) _____

Children (toys, insurance, sports, travel, camp, clothes, education, allowance) _____

Medication / supplements / doctor visits (what your insurance does not cover) _____

Credit cards (monthly payments) _____

Monthly Expense Total _____

Monthly Income Total _____

Ways to Reduce Monthly Expenses

Gasoline - Ride a bike or walk. Use public transportation. Car pool. Limit the number of miles you drive monthly, drive the speed limit, and never exceed sixty miles an hour. Purchase a vehicle that runs on diesel and convert to vegetable oil.

Car Payment - Purchase used vehicles rather than new ones. Better deals are found when purchasing from individuals rather than dealerships. Think of your car as utilitarian and not an expression of manhood or financial status.

Car Maintenance - Keep up with basic service. Regular oil changes, tire pressure checks and tune-ups extend the longevity of your automobile. Stay away from vehicle luxuries such as stereo systems, alarms and mechanical enhancements. These acquisitions make your vehicle more vulnerable to theft, subject to a higher rate of insurance and expensive maintenance costs.

Travel Expenses - Limit travel excursions. If possible take your own food when traveling. Spend more time enjoying the outdoors rather then paying for entertainment or theme parks.

Hunt only for food. Leave modern all-terrain vehicles at home. Level the playing field by hunting with a bow and arrow and tracking instead of baiting an animal. Hunt with respect knowing that any adult animal you decide to kill has a mate and family that he or she provides for.

Hunt the sick and elderly as opposed to the strongest members of a herd which diminishes the health and stability of that population. Hunting the strongest and most beautiful is usually for the notoriety of the kill or for the trophy of hide and head. Imagine your own head hanging on a wall, your body stuffed in a museum, or your skin stretched flat under a coffee table.

Insurance - Carry the minimum amount of insurance as required by law on your vehicle. Invest in your health by exercising, eating organic whole foods, and refer to homeopathic manuals for minor complaints. Refrain from purchasing flashy vehicles, trendy and valuable possessions or furnishings to avoid thievery.

Mortgage or Rent - Purchase smaller older homes. If buying a home will put you further in debt, consider renting. Renters are free to leave when necessary, not responsible for structural or appliance repairs and do not pay taxes.

House Cleaner - Clean your own house. Small living spaces adorned with few possessions require less time to clean.

Gardner /Lawn Care / Pesticides - Plant, mow, and weed your own property. If you can't push mow your property with a manual mower requiring neither gasoline or electricity, it is too big. Deal with pests in non-poisonous or lethal ways.

Home Repair - Keep the home small to eliminate repair costs. Check out books from your local library on how to make household repairs yourself. The less you have, the less you have to maintain.

Electricity - Do away with electrical kitchen appliances. (Storage space will increase as a result.) Use hand tools instead of electric ones. Use fans instead of air conditioners. Do away with the television or limit to one hour a day. Utilize computers at the library. Turn off lights when not in use. When we have minimal electrical devices, sustainable energy such as solar power becomes easy to accomplish and very affordable.

Natural Gas or Propane - Gas appliances are more economical than electric ones. Keep thermostats turned off while at work and at bedtime.

Water / Sewage / Garbage - Take four minute showers by timing yourself with an egg timer. Landscape with native plants that are drought resistant. Use water from washing up to water plants. Set up a water catch system such as a rain barrel or cistern. Flush your toilets only when necessary. Purchase items with minimal packaging. Compost food waste. Recycle glass, aluminum, tin, plastic, paper and cardboard.

Phone - Try living without a phone or answering machine. Utilize a landline instead of an electronic phone. The line will be clearer, and in weather emergencies, a landline can still function in the event of a power loss.

Cell Phone - Eliminate cell phones. In doing so, you obliterate possible health risks and the environmental hazards associated with disposal.

Storage Unit - If you do not have room for acquired possessions residing in a storage unit, weed and sell the contents.

Alarm Systems - Don't purchase fashionable and valuable items.

Groceries - Shop once a month and support your local farmer's market. Limit your meat intake to once a week or try to forego it altogether. Consume organic whole foods such as vegetables and fruit. Stay away from junk food and pre-prepared foods. Plant a garden and grow your own food.

Childcare - If your living costs are minimal, it becomes possible for one parent to be at home with small children.

Magazines / Newspapers / Books - Cancel all subscriptions. Read magazines, newspapers and check out books from your neighborhood library.

Cigarettes - Quit smoking or chewing. This could take a year or more to do. If you can reduce your usage each time you embark on a smoke out, eventually you will reach a place where you no longer want or need to smoke.

Alcohol - Limit your alcohol consumption to special occasions only. Purchase alcohol at a liquor store rather than drinking at bars or restaurants.

Coffee - Make your own coffee at home. Have coffee out only on special occasions. Consume regular blends as opposed to specialty coffees.

Videos - Limit your viewing to one video per week.

Cable / Internet - Consider reading instead of watching television. Use the Internet at the library.

Computers - Engage kids in outdoor activities instead of electronic entertainment. Instead of purchasing CD's, listen to the radio.

Sports - Gather weekly to play sports with friends. Attend local high school and college games, rather than professional ones. Plan to eat at home before or after the game.

Entertainment - Attend special events once a month. Dine at home rather than eating out.

Eating Out - Dine out only three times a month at reasonably priced restaurants. Support local establishments rather than fast food or chain operations. Establish weekly neighborhood potlucks.

Spa or Gym Memberships - Eliminate gym memberships. Walk or ride your bike to work. Daily work in a garden also provides a great source of exercise.

Instructional Classes - Limit classes or activities for adults and children to one per week.

Jewelry / Home Accessories - Live without body adornments or purchase used items from second hand stores. Change home accessories only if something is beyond repair. Refrain from accumulating time saving gadgets.

Clothes - Purchase clothes at second hand stores or garage sales and create your own style. Wear every day clothes as opposed to special gear for cycling or sports.

Shoes - Purchase well-made shoes that can be repaired.

Hair - Cut your own hair. Refrain from chemical treatments, perms or dyes.

Manicures / Pedicures / Tattoos - Live without body art or indulge only on special occasions.

Cosmetics - Limit cosmetics to lipstick, shampoo, lotion and soap. Avoid plastic surgery or other youth enhancing products. One way to develop appreciation for your own natural beauty and the aging process is to avoid watching television, Hollywood blockbusters and reading fashion magazines. Check out yoga magazines for an alternative look at beauty and how to grow old gracefully.

Pets / Livestock - Limit your household to one pet such as a cat or dog. Neuter or spay your pet. Adopt a pet from your local animal shelter. Do not adopt animals such as birds, snakes, lizards, fish, ferrets, etc. These exotic species belong in the wild and not in your living room.

ॐ

The local animal shelter in my community (around 40,000 people) puts down over five thousand animals a year and secures adoptions for less than eight hundred animals a year. If you are unable to commit the money, time and space necessary to care for animals, pets and livestock should be avoided.

Children - Plan for pregnancy or adoption. Be prepared for the necessary time commitment to raise a child. If you have children, consider letting them carry the responsibility of their own interests and needs. It is the best way to teach children how to manage their money and their appetites. Children could contribute to the cost of family vacations and work for privileges beyond shelter and food while living at home with their parents.

Medication / Supplements / Doctors - Avoid seeing a doctor unless it is an emergency. Improve your health with exercise and proper diet. Visit a health food store to learn how to diagnose and heal simple ailments on your own.

Credit Cards - Have only one credit card. Pay it off at the end of every month. Never carry a balance.

Money - Live without or pay as you go. Save ten percent of all income. Trade service for service or item for item.

Debt - Cancel your credit cards. Pay cash for everything. Set up a payment plan with the help of a financial consultant.

Review your monthly expense chart. Circle three or more expenses and commit to modifying them.

Our lifestyle invokes many questions. I hope that you will take the time to answer these questions and then initiate further discussion with family and friends.

How much time do you spend at work each week?

How much time do you spend finishing office work at home?

Do you have more than one job?

Does your job entail working with hazardous materials? If so, do you feel your health is being compromised as a result?

Do you work for a company that has had questions raised about its management of people, production or natural resources? If so, how does this affect you?

Did you take your present job based on your passion for the work involved or for the salary you receive?

Do you wake up every day dreading the hours you must put in at work? If so, why?

What is your dream job? Are you doing that? And if not, why aren't you?

❧

During adolescence we tend to dream big and sometimes our parents, educators, or other mentors cannot fathom our vision at that age. With good intentions, they redirect us onto a more secure and financially viable path. Oftentimes, we ourselves get in the way of our dreams. We become frightened of an outcome we can't possibly predict, and so, we settle for a path that has already been well proven.

List three things you wish you had more time for.

Why don't you have the time to pursue these interests?

❧

Our lifestyle drives everything. Truthfully, we own nothing. It all owns us. The burden of expenses and material possessions determines how hard we work and our quality of life. The less you have to maintain, the more money and time you will possess.

Bees

While transplanting lavender to a sunnier location, sweat trickled down my back, tickling the space above my sacrum. As I punched the dirt down, a distant hum vibrated the air around me. I imagined cobblestone pathways leading into and away from the center of my garden. I sat back on my heels, the vibration intensifying as I wiped the sweat from my face. Hundreds of bees swarmed around me as they feasted on the nectar of blanket flower, soapwort, iris, snapdragon, purple coneflower, Mexican hat, primrose and delphinium. I had been so engrossed in my work that I hadn't noticed I was toiling in their midst. When did they arrive? How long had they been here? I watched as they stumbled into the center of their desire and then buzzed off to another destination.

How easily we all managed to share the space and continue with our work. I didn't bother them and they didn't bother me.

Shopping

More than any other time in history,
mankind faces a crossroads.
One path leads to despair and utter hopelessness.
The other to total extinction.
Let us pray we have the wisdom
to choose correctly.

- Woody Allen

Where do you shop most frequently and why? (besides grocery stores)

What do you shop for most often?

What are your impulse buys?

Why do you shop? How does it make you feel?

Do you shop because you are bored?

Do you shop more frequently at big box stores or local businesses?

Is there anything else that could replace shopping as a past time?

Are you familiar with the tax breaks, human rights abuses and environmental neglect that benefit American corporations setting up business in poor countries? Does this affect you in any way?

Does the loss of green space and wilderness areas within our cities and towns have anything to do with our desire to shop?

Black Widow

I sat on my friend's porch drinking in the warmth of mountain sunshine. As we talked I noticed a small red knot below my anklebone aggravated by the strap of my sandal. My foot swelled accompanied by shooting pain.

When I awakened the following morning, the room spun around me as if I were trapped in a kaleidoscope. Overcome with dizziness, I forced my feet to the floor. Gripping the staircase rail, a thousand pins and needles pierced my skin, sweat drained from my pores, nausea bubbled up in my esophagus and I became light as air.

Later a doctor would conclude that the symptoms were that of a Black Widow bite. The feeling of drunkenness lingered and vertigo was my bedside companion for weeks after.

Black Widows dangle in doorframes, under logs and sometimes in the blades of grass. These small spiders can kill pets and children with their venomous bites, cause serious illness and on rare occasion, neurological damage in adults.

Nietzsche said it best,
"What doesn't kill me makes me stronger."

Celebration

*Everything that has a beginning
has an ending.
Make peace with that and all will be well.*

\- Buddha

We spend a great deal of time throughout the year shopping for specific days of celebration. Some alternative ways to celebrate days normally associated with gift giving and different approaches to specific traditions will be discussed in this chapter. These ideas may or may not be suitable to your life. The purpose is to inspire you to create your own reformations. How do we celebrate and live so that we generate less waste and at the same time avoid financial debt?

Birthdays - Prepare a great meal and desert to share with family and friends. The gift could be a story from each guest about a specific experience shared with the birthday person.

Graduation - A celebration with delicious food, family and friends. Rather than bestowing gifts, roast the honoree by sharing humorous tales about the graduate's life.

Weddings - Wear clothes that you can wear at other times in your life. Instead of purchasing gifts, let friends and family help you with the cost of the wedding. For example, it is possible that friends or family have gardens or land that would be the perfect setting for a wedding. Family and friends could donate the flowers from their gardens, prepare unique dishes of food, play music or take photographs.

❧

Two friends of mine married about fifteen years ago. They hired a judge to perform the ceremony, drove off into the wilderness where they hiked out to a beautiful spot and then exchanged marriage vows. The total cost amounted to the officiary's fee plus the expense of gasoline. A lovely and meaningful ceremony generating very little waste.

Valentines - Historically this day has been a celebration of love. Instead of the ordinary diamonds, flowers or chocolate, create a valentine that contains only the gift of your words.

৵

Over the years my partners have blessed me with lovely tokens of their affection and yet it is only their letters and poems that I keep. It needn't rhyme or be flowery in nature, but only ring of authenticity. Someone once wrote,

> *"I was thinking about the years I've known you
> and how much I admired you from the start and
> how much I admire what you've become.
> You remain without parallel,
> the thing I love most in this world."*

Material possessions lose their meaning and place in our lives, but testimonies of love survive separation and, ultimately, even death. They linger beyond the scope of our own lives, to penetrate the hearts of those we leave behind.

Thanksgiving - While this is a day of feasting and giving thanks for many, for some native people, this is a day of mourning. Instead of feasting, perhaps we could fast and reflect on how to live with more integrity and honor in our dealings with others.

The next two days of celebration are traditional Christian holidays. However, in the United States these celebrations are for many secular as opposed to religious holidays and are celebrated by Hindus, Muslims, Jews and others.

Easter - I have a friend who is the youngest of ten children born into a family with strong cultural ties to Norway and Sweden. Feeding ten children was quite a challenge so oatmeal was a popular meal. They saved the oatmeal containers and used them to make their own Easter baskets utilizing materials found only in the house. It became an exercise in imagination and design. It was so successful that the eldest sibling now in her sixties, the youngest in her forties, and all those in-between still to this day make their own Easter baskets.

Christmas - Several years ago, I approached my family and friends with this idea:

"You know, I really don't need anything. And, I don't think you need anything either. Could our gift to each other be the celebration of our family and friendship with great food and great conversation?"

Another approach might be to draw names between family members so that only one gift is given and one gift is received. In order to reduce waste, wrap the gifts in newspapers or other recyclable materials. Buy used merchandise and limit gift dollar amount. The whole process could be an adventure, riddled with humor, creativity and resourcefulness.

Acts of service can be an exceptional and meaningful gift at any time of the year for any occasion. Sometimes, people need someone to talk to, someone to prepare them a good meal, or help with grocery shopping, raking leaves, etc. There is no greater gift than to gift yourself and time to someone else.

New Year's and Independence Days - Create a ritual or ceremony to give thanks for blessings received in the past year.

Friends and neighbors could gather on these days to reflect on the past year's events. Commit to living more mindfully in the year to come. Resolutions could be made and shared by community members to become a zero waste neighborhood. In the process, community and family ties are deepened.

List three days of celebration that you would like to recreate in your own families.

Education - Home schooling is a great way to educate your children. You can foster the natural gifts of your child that the public and private schools don't have the time or resources to do.

Consider educating yourself rather than seeking a college education. Take classes specific to your interest through a non-degree program, read, apprentice yourself to someone, learn a trade, travel, live and work abroad while you learn another language or just focus on creating a work situation around whatever engages your passion.

૭

I went into debt twenty-five thousand dollars when

I returned to school for my Masters degree. I would never encourage anyone to seek an education through a university that they couldn't pay for outright. One of the fastest growing trends in the United States, are twenty four year olds exiting college fifty thousand dollars in debt. This is a lifetime debt that they will not likely pay off until they are well into their fifties. As a result many of these students are returning home to live with their parents.

Another scenario is that some people train for a specific career only to discover upon graduating they can no longer pursue that dream because it will not generate enough funds to pay for their student loans. A monthly payment for loans totaling fifty thousand dollars can be six hundred to a thousand dollars or more. This one bill doesn't cover shelter, food costs or transportation. In many ways the high cost of education destroys dreams as well.

Funerals - While I was in graduate school, I had a boyfriend from Iran. Amir was in medical school when his father passed away and could not return to Iran for political reasons. The family made a video of the funeral, and I was fortunate to view this with him.

His father died at home in Tehran, and the body remained in the home so that the family could prepare the body for burial. After the body was wrapped in a light muslin shroud, family and friends gathered at the house for the visitation and wake. Then Amir's father was carried on a stretcher by family members from the house to the cemetery. While some dug the grave, others sang. After placing the body in the grave, one family member climbed into the grave to gently rock Amir's father as they sang to him one last time. The body was covered and the family returned home: no fancy caskets, no embalming, no make-up, no special clothes, no funeral homes, no flowers.

Population - Unfortunately, there is no shortage of human beings on this planet. There are millions and millions of children orphaned by war, poverty and disaster. We have to rethink what it means to have a family. Is it possible to create a family that does not carry our bloodlines but carries the seeds of our love instead?

Automobile - I gave up my vehicle the last year I spent in New Mexico. When I no longer had this huge chunk of metal parked in the driveway, my view of the world broadened.

ॐ

Riding my bike full time was not easy in arid country, seven thousand feet above sea level. Acclimating to this new form of transportation meant I had to endure weeks of fatigue and pain until I developed the muscle to handle this new lifestyle. There was no need for a gym membership because I was getting plenty of exercise. The expenses associated with my truck (insurance, registration, maintenance, gasoline) all fell by the wayside. My desire to accumulate possessions also dissipated because I had no way of getting things larger than two grocery bags to and from my house. All of this equated to more money for my household.

But the real gift of letting go of my truck became the ride itself. Once I developed the muscle, not only did I never want to own a vehicle again, I didn't want to ride in one either. On my bike I took in everything around me: the smell of Russian olive trees in spring, pastures full of wild irises, redwing blackbirds perched on the cattails in the meadows, the smell of piñon smoke and roasting chilies, riding through golden cottonwood leaves and speaking to my neighbors as they worked in their gardens or sat on their porches. I learned to read the sky as weather systems formed over the mountains. Since I no longer desired speed, a certain peace and calmness took over my life. Even though my world had shrunk in terms of geography, my immediate world expanded, teeming with wildlife, song, beauty and physical joy.

The bicycle I ride was purchased in 1992. I tune the bike up annually which costs me around thirty-five dollars. It is a Raleigh mountain bike with eighteen gears, of which I only use about three.

Vulture

The Bosque is a tangled web of life and death. Meandering through the dead and dying, my eyes followed youthful limbs as they pierced the canopy above me where large black birds swooped in and out of view. Their very presence signifies a death, and in Egyptian mythology, they were responsible for carrying the souls of the dead into the next world.

It wasn't long after that, while riding my bike before day breaks, out of mist and darkness emerged five vultures roosting at the top of a tree. My breath caught in my throat, the sight, ghastly and ominous. Later, I confided in a friend that I feared it was a premonition of death. She dismissed my interpretation and advised me not to read into such events.

I continued to see them, while lying in my hammock, and once while camping they flew straight through the campsite. The sound of their wings fluttering down my spine with a shiver.

Upon my return, there was a message from my mother requesting I come home. Six weeks later, the soul of my father was carried over.

Offerings

Clutter

*The spiritual can never be attained until
materiality is gone.*

- Swami Vivekenanda

Offerings

While there are usually good intentions behind gift giving, it often leads to substantial clutter in our homes, garages, closets, attics and basements. Sometimes we even rent a storage unit just to store more stuff.

Stuff is created from raw and live materials found on and in the earth. In speaking so irreverently about material things we foster an attitude that all things are replaceable and certainly not equal to human life.

Clutter jams the life. Excessive material possessions leads to chaos, obstruction, confusion and imbalance in our homes. People can't part with their possessions, so they end up tiptoeing around them, tripping over them, blocking windows and doors with them, imprisoned by stuff.

What possessions do you have that clutter your life? (Too many tools, too many shoes, an old vehicle on the property?)

What keeps you from letting go of things?

☙

During a trip abroad, I worked as a house painter to help pay for my travel expenses. My bosses were immigrants themselves who both worked in health care. Camela was a nurse and Grey was a psychologist.

The old, Victorian house, originally Grey's first home, was now being renovated for future use as a holiday rental. The three outbuildings on the property overflowed with miscellaneous objects that had accumulated over the last decade. We discovered about six lawn mowers, some overgrown with weeds while others were buried under piles of building materials in different sheds on the property.

The next morning I looked out the window and thought I was hallucinating when I saw more lawn mowers.

"I thought we took those mowers to the dump?"

"We did," sighed Camela. "These are different mowers I found this morning."

"He had twelve mowers?"

"This is nothing. There are probably fifteen mowers in and around our barn at the other house."

"Why does he keep buying them?"

"Grey thinks he'll fix them and then resell them."

"How many has he resold?"

"Zero."

ঌ

Most of the time we don't let go of things because we think, some day we might need them. This may be true of some things but it is not true for most. We may have particular difficulty letting go of gifts or heirlooms but if these items are not being used or stored in boxes out of view, consider selling or re-gifting them.

We often hear,

"Don't worry if it breaks, we can always get a new one."

A good question to pose before we purchase anything,

"Is it possible to keep and maintain this for a lifetime?"

৶

Our ancestors left us beautiful paintings on the inner faces of caves. We can only wonder about their significance. Most often, the images are of animals or humans with animal characteristics. Perhaps they had great reverence for creatures responsible in providing them with necessary food and clothing. Perhaps they were offerings to delight a spirit greater than themselves. These paintings are all that remains of our ancestors' time here.

The people who follow in our footsteps will find rusted metal skeletons, oil drums oozing nuclear waste, streams running foul and blackened water, earth splitting apart with plastic and a horizon dominated by steel, glass, asphalt and concrete. Is this to be our legacy?

Make it an annual event to go through everything you own and weed out unwanted possessions. If you plan on giving items to friends or family members, be sure to ask them first, to gauge if they actually need it or plan on using it. If not, consider selling the items or donating them to local charities, Goodwill or Salvation Army.

If you have allowed things to accumulate, you may want to go through your possessions every six months.

A serious but contemporary dilemma with accumulation is that some people have difficulty parting with anything regardless of its use or value. One way to approach this is to hire someone who will come to your home, help you sort through your possessions and then ask tough questions regarding your desire to keep it all.

But the best way to deal with accumulation is to just stop accumulating. One way to stop accumulating is to never buy anything on impulse. Always return home and think about the acquisition. Ask yourself, where you are going to put it? What items will you displace in the process? What are you going to do with these old items? Do you have the money to make this purchase or will this be on credit? And most importantly, do you really need it?

Another way to stop accumulating is to stop obligatory gift giving between family and friends. I realize this is a sensitive topic, but ask yourself - do you really need anything? If you are saying no to that question, chances are everyone in your immediate circle of friends and family are saying no to that question. It really does warrant a conversation between family and friends, so that we can stop filling up landfills and second hand stores. Start new traditions that keep us from polluting the planet and destroying our own health in the process.

Gifting could be a spontaneous and meaningful act, exercised on rare and exceptional occasion.

List three things that you will find new homes for by the end of the month.

ॐ

Not so long ago, I thought about all the things I had ever owned from the moment I arrived on the planet: baby bottles, diapers, toys and clothes, bikes and cars, furniture and accessories. I realized it is all still here. It may have been relocated, someone else may be using some of it, but most of it is buried in a landfill or dumped at the bottom of the ocean, but it is still on the planet. If we didn't have the option to dispose of anything and we had to live with it for the rest of our lives, we would become quite careful in our accumulation of anything.

In Albuquerque, several environmentalists decided to test the water. They took their samples where the water exits the water treatment plant. They looked at over one hundred and twenty substances, and the number one substance found in the water was caffeine, a result of all the caffeinated drinks we consume. Some of the other substances identified were flame-retardants, fertilizers, pesticides, herbicides (from all the chemicals we dump on our lawns), prescription and over the counter drugs. It's all still here - even what we eat and drink is still here. There is no away.

Ant

Several years ago I visited my mother when dogwood blossoms brighten hollows of pine and oak trees.

One morning following an ugly confrontation over the poisoning of fire ants, I escaped outdoors to bask in the shimmering beauty of mulberry blossoms, full on pink. Light scattered across the pavement as I noticed a trail of ants crossing the grass, marching onto the driveway, continuing up the frame of the garage to where I couldn't see. I leaned my head in close to the line of ants marching in both directions and whispered,

"If you guys don't leave the premises, my mother is going to dump poison all over you."

I moved back indoors, hoping she would not venture outside. Anxiety mounted as I pictured the gruesome death that accompanies poison. Restless, I slipped out the back entrance to check on the situation.

The driveway, the grass, the frame of the garage, stood completely barren. Not one ant in sight anywhere.

Offerings

Beauty

We have no art.
We simply do everything as beautifully as we can.

- Balinese Proverb

When our lives are devoid of clutter, order prevails. Order provides pathways, balance, clarity and space. Nothing new can come into our lives unless there is space for it.

I'm not speaking about material objects here. I'm speaking about a new job, a new way of thinking, a new way of living. It is in order that beauty is discovered.

If you ask people to talk about a moment when they experienced profound beauty- it almost always occurs in nature… breath taking beauty… beauty so powerful, that it lifts us right out of our struggles. It is this mystery of natural forces that can lead us into a creative life.

Whose style do you buy into and why? (Nike, Calvin Klein, John Deere, Martha Stewart , etc.)

What kind of car do you drive and why?

What does your car say about you?

How many gasoline powered machines do you own? (RV's, campers, all-terrain vehicles, lawn mowers, boats, motorcycles, leaf blowers, jet skis, snowmobiles, tractors, chain saws)

What is the square footage of your house? How many people could conceivably live there?

⁊

When I lived in the mountains I had a friend from Honduras who had been in the United States for only six months. Jovanni spoke very little English. I agreed to help him with his English if he would assist me with my Spanish. Our first lesson took place at my residence that was a one-room three hundred square foot cottage. Jovani couldn't believe what a beautiful house I lived in.

"It would be nice if it were bigger, though. I think it's too small, even for one person."

"Too small?"

He scrunched up his face in disbelief. He then went on to say that six people could live in this dwelling very comfortably. He even showed me how the room could accommodate six sleepers.

I stood there with my mouth open, thinking, SIX PEOPLE LIVING HERE? Then it hit me. I was obnoxiously rich.

Is your home a sustainable structure constructed out
of adobe, cob or straw bale? Does it utilize alternative
energy sources, such as solar power or wind power? Does
it have a water catch system, cistern, grey water system,
composting toilet or outhouse?

How many cell phones do you own or have previously
owned? How many hours a day do you spend chatting?

How many televisions do you own? How many hours a
day do you spend watching?

How many computers do you own? How many hours a
day do you spend online?

How often do you exchange the entire system for a new
one?

ॐ

In the summer of 2006 I took my Macintosh Power Book 2000 in to be upgraded. The salesman practically laughed me out of the store.

"This is ridiculous! Just buy a new one!"

"Well, wait just a minute!" I lamented.

"There are three hundred million people in this country. Let's just say they all have a computer and then let's say they all get a new one every two or three years. Where do all those used computers go?"

The salesman went over to his own computer, punched in some information and then brought up a pair of photographs. He turned to me and said,

"Right there - to huge landfills in Africa and China."

I felt so ignorant for not knowing that. These landfills were crawling with poor people; adults and children stripping the metal from the boards to be sold at market. Computer boards are highly toxic and not only pose a danger to the environment but to those who come into contact with them. Awakened, I said,

"I don't think I can support that."

Remorseless, and untouched, his final words reverberated in my chest.

"It's just the cost of doing business."

Economics without spirituality can give you temporary and physical gratification but it cannot provide an internal fulfillment. Spiritual economics brings service, compassion, and relationships into equal play with profit and efficiency. We need them both and we need them simultaneously.

- E. F. Schumacher

ತ್ಠಾ

Electronic waste amounts to seventy percent of the toxic garbage found in America's landfills. In 2003, three billion tons of electronic waste were generated just in the United States.

How much lead is in an iPod? What is the mercury content in a cell phone? What are the hazards of flame-retardants in computer boards?

Electronic devices or cancer free children?
Cell phones or mercury free drinking water?
Computers or fewer landfills?
Automobiles or arctic ice caps, polar bears and beluga whales?

How do you connect to nature on a daily basis and how many hours a day do you spend in nature?

Name ten wild creatures that are native to the area in which you live? How often do you see these animals?

How are you creative? What do you design or make regularly? How many hours a day do you spend in creativity?

Can you or your children build a shelter, plant a garden, hunt without contemporary weapons or identify edible plants in the wild?

Take a moment and compare the number of hours spent watching television and on the computer with the number of hours spent in nature and creativity.

ॐ

Some might say that when we are wealthy, we tend to pay others to be creative for us, and when we are poor; we tend to be very creative and resourceful because we have no other options. However, when there is a lack of reverence and connection with nature, people stop creating.

Horse

Shortly after I moved into my country cottage, a gentleman began boarding his two horses in the pasture adjacent to the property I lived on. The owner, on meeting me, threw a saddle over the fence and suggested I ride whenever I wanted. I began by riding the gelding but, in the end, preferred the red stallion whose gentle disposition, keen intelligence and graceful form would on occasion bring me to tears.

I saddled up Horse on a crisp, fall afternoon. We slowly poked down the dirt road that led from the barn to the Bosque taking in the seasonal smell of wood smoke, apples and chilies. Ahead, the path was dotted with small children. Every year, the local farmer opened his apple orchards to the community for the experience of picking apples.

A group of stragglers, heard our impending arrival, turned quickly in our direction, and set off running towards us. Sitting atop this two thousand pound stud horse, I panicked when Horse abruptly stopped, ears straightened, nostrils flared and a deep, disturbing, rumble vibrated throughout his body.

Eight children screaming with delight flung their bodies around his legs, crawled under his belly and nestled their faces into his coat. Horse didn't budge, didn't falter, didn't so much as shift his weight. He simply smelled the tops of their gleeful heads.

He knew before I did. He sensed their innocence. As the adults raced towards them with concern, I peered into shining faces characterized by Down syndrome.

Solutions

Hope is where your ass is.

- Phillip Berrigan

How can we be part of the solution?

Water Bottles - Purchase your own permanent water bottle and fill up before you leave the house.

~

Between the shores of North America and Japan floats the Eastern Garbage Patch. This floating trash dump is two times the size of Texas and ninety percent of its' content is plastic. A great example of community action is San Francisco's proposed legislation to do away with bottled water. Many restaurants have already removed bottled water from their menus as a show of support.

Coffee Cups - Take your own cup when purchasing coffee to go. Look at it for what it is - you are drinking coffee out of a tree or out of the dregs of an oil barrel.

Paper Products - Use cloth napkins, cloth towels, handkerchiefs, cloth diapers, real plates. Don't kill a forest just to have a party.

Cloth Bags - Take your own reusable bags to any and all stores that you patronize.

~

The United States uses thirty billion plastic bags each year which require twelve million barrels of oil for their manufacture. One plastic bag could spend two hundred years in nature before decomposition. Legislation has been passed by the community of San Francisco to eliminate plastic bags in the market place.

Take Out - Avoid take-out.

~

Most of the trash that lines our city streets and roadways is from fast food restaurants. We could eliminate all the bottles and cans alongside roads if there were a bottle/can deposit.

Green Cleaners - Switch over to cruel- free and environmentally friendly cleaners.

~

Many people believe that big industry is responsible for most of our pollution. If you look under your kitchen sink, in your utility rooms and in your garages, you will find a variety of weapons of mass destruction: poisons, herbicides, bleach, fabric softeners, harsh detergents, etc. If every household uses similar products, multiply that by the number of households in your town, and you have an outrageous amount of toxicity flowing through your water system everyday.

Pesticides - Poisons are deadly to all who come into contact with them. Practice living with the species you don't like as opposed to eliminating them.

~

Honey Bees are responsible for one-third of all the foods we eat. Colonies of bees are collapsing across the nation and beekeepers believe that pesticide is the culprit. These new pesticides are designed to break down the immune system, cause memory loss and nervous system disorders.

Supposedly these pesticides are safe for humans and animals but deadly to insects. Bees exposed to these pesticides lose their sense of navigation and never return to the hive. If the die off continues, most beekeepers will

Offerings

be out of business and this may spell out the demise of the American food supply.

Instead of honoring the wisdom of beekeepers by banning the use of these pesticides, which would protect the health of honeybees and the food supply, we must wait for laboratory scientists to determine the absolute cause for colony collapse. This could take years.

Strange that common illnesses plaguing humans are immune and nervous system disorders, as well as memory loss. Perhaps this is why we too, have lost our own sense of navigation in the world.

Perfumes - Go fragrance free.

ے

The most common form of air pollution that we encounter daily are perfumes. Perfumes are in laundry detergents, fabric softeners, air fresheners, cleaning products, incense, scented candles, pot pouri, cosmetics, and colognes.

Electricity - Reduce your own usage of electricity.

ے

Eighteen power plants are scheduled to be built in the state of Texas. No one wants these monstrosities sitting in their backyards. Be a part of the solution and reduce your own usage of electricity.

Porch lights, security lights, Christmas lights, computers, televisions, air conditioners, dishwashers, kitchen appliances, tools, electronic devices and signs - turn them off.

Travel and Tourism - Travel to local destinations and refrain from visiting tourist attractions such as wildlife habitats or breeding grounds.

Travel green by leaving all of your electronics at home including your cameras. Carry your own water bottles and coffee cups. Pack one small bag that you can carry onto the plane and put under the seat in front of you. Once there, continue your travels by foot, bicycle or public transportation.

੨৺

The best gift we could give ourselves and to those remaining species struggling to survive alongside us, is to just leave them alone.

Pets - Pick up after your pets.

੨৺

3.6 billion pounds of dog waste is produced in the United States annually. That's equivalent to eight hundred football fields, one foot high. Over two million tons of cat litter is deposited in city landfills each year. The urine and feces from household pets are known to contaminate city watersheds, rivers and streams in close proximity to our cities and towns. Next to humans, cats and dogs are the next serious threat to wildlife and the environment.

Fireworks - Celebrate in silence and stillness.

੨৺

Millions of taxpayer's dollars are spent annually on public firework displays. Imagine if that money were allocated to serve the needs of the community instead. Small business loans, mentorship programs for teens and parenting classes would benefit far more citizens than ten minutes of bang. Our streets and psyches would benefit as well from less noise, less litter, fewer injuries and fires.

Charities - Solve the problems in your own communities first.

❧

We have no way of knowing if the aid we send ever arrives to those it is promised to. A friend, who lived in Africa for four years, related that aid sent in the form of money, in many cases, is not received by those in need. Sacks of grain donated by the United States with Uncle Sam's picture on the front end up for sale in local food stores and mosquito nets sent to keep African children from contracting malaria become fishing nets.

If you're interested in giving, give to your local charities where you can at least follow the result of your cash gift. Local charities often overlooked and under funded are women's shelters, boys and girls clubs, animal shelters and medical care for the poor.

Shopping - Buy used.

❧

But when you must buy new, support your local businesses rather than corporate chain stores.

Children - Teach your children to care for each other and all species that inhabit this earth. Teach them to live with less stuff. Teach your children to be responsible members of their communities and to resolve conflicts by peaceful means.

❧

Encourage your children to tackle the problems in their own communities. Whether it is issues of litter, cleaning up streams and public lands, inventing new uses for items deemed garbage or accompanying their parents to town meetings, demonstrations or political rallies. There is absolutely no voice more powerful in government than that of children.

Create rites of passage to acknowledge turning points in the life. In some indigenous tribes, young people not initiated into adulthood by their elders are considered adolescents their entire lives. The elders of a family could create a series of tasks to be completed over the course of a year by thirteen year olds or at the onset of puberty to prepare the child for adulthood.

List three or more habits that you want to reform in your own life.

Don't look for big things,
just do small things with great love.

- Mother Teresa

❧

Change the dream from a demonstrative life burdened by material possessions to a life of simplicity and humility.

Every time you get into your car or truck from this moment on, think how your life might be different without it. There are roughly five hundred million cars in the world and two hundred and forty million are in the United States.

There is not enough time to reconfigure the entire

automobile industry. The automobile is one of the major producers of greenhouse gases that result in global warming. We can drive ourselves into extinction or we could learn to live without it.

Holland has a population of sixteen million and hence sixteen million bicycles travel the roads. The mayor of Paris is widening sidewalks, expanding green spaces, restricting traffic to one lane in some places as well as closing some streets to traffic altogether. Denmark has ten thousand kilometers of established bike paths throughout the country. In Portland, Oregon - ten thousand commuters cross the Hawthorne and Sellwood bridges on their bicycles everyday. It can happen.

Many of you are thinking, these problems are just too big, changing my life couldn't possibly make a difference. We can either throw up our hands in exhaustion and prepare for the end or we can adjust to the changing tide and see this for what it is. Changing our lifestyle is a matter of imagination and will; the task before us is a phenomenal opportunity to be extraordinarily creative.

Raven

When I left New York City, I wanted a definitive ceremony, a rite of passage. I chose a sixteen-day white water trip, paddling two hundred and twenty-five miles through the Grand Canyon.

The first day on the river was grey and rainy, the water temperature registered forty-five degrees. Paddling without rain gear, the freezing water broke over my body for six hours before we set up camp. The cold had permeated my bones, leaving me brittle and broken. I climbed into my sleeping bag defeated. My teeth rattled the death march as clouds passed in front of the moon. I drifted in and out of sleep as the guide's warning played continuously through my dreams.

"The only way out of here - is by helicopter."

The next morning, sunlight crept down the canyon walls. I crawled out of my bedroll with a heavy heart.

"Only fifteen days to go."

I grabbed some breakfast and headed down to the river where a log, stretching into the sunshine beckoned me. Raven perched on a nearby cliff, spread her wings and landed a few feet from where I now sat. I commended Raven for her boldness.

I put a piece of sausage an arm's length away. She hopped onto the log, sidestepped across and then gobbled it down as she returned. Bewildered, I appealed to my fellow campers,

"Are these birds tame?"

One guide remarked,

"Never seen anything like it."

It was the beginning of an incredible journey.

Offerings

Reverence

*We must recover the sense of majesty of the creation
and the ability to be worshipful in its presence
- for it is only on the condition of humility
and reverence for the world that our species
will be able to remain in it.*

- Wendell Berry

What do we have reverence for in this culture?

We certainly have great reverence for money simply demonstrated by what people are willing to do for it. Not to mention all the opportunities to win money through lotteries, casinos and /or game shows. We have tremendous reverence for machinery, especially our automobiles, and an alarming reverence for violence.

We spend billions of dollars annually to be entertained by violence either through the Internet, television, films, music, video games, magazines, literature and/or sports.

We spend over two hundred million dollars a day on the war in Iraq which doesn't include the cost of the war in Afghanistan or the cost of other conflicts the United States is presently engaged in around the world.

More than three women a day are murdered at the hands of their husbands and/or boyfriends in the United States.

The leading cause of death for pregnant women in the United States is homicide.

Females disappear everyday in the United States.

*A nation is not conquered until
the hearts of its women are on the ground.
Then it is finished, no matter how brave its warriors
or how strong its weapons.*

- Cheyenne Proverb

How do we demonstrate our reverence for the earth and other species?

When we consider the nature of zoos, wildlife parks, trophy hunting, factory farms, rodeos, marine parks, horse racing, circus acts, aquariums, dog racing, exotic pets, animal laboratory experimentation, dog fighting, genetic plant and animal engineering, cock fighting, ski resorts, amusement parks, water parks, four wheeling, extreme sports, logging, oil drilling and mining; it appears that we are only interested in the enslavement of the natural world for the amusement and progress of people.

The greatness of a nation and its moral progress
can be judged by the way it treats its animals.

\- Gandhi

Why do people feel entitled to kill wilderness and wildlife?

Where do the roots of this privilege originate?

ॐ

Everything on this planet lives at the mercy of human beings. Aquatic biologist, Betsy Smith says,

"Even animals know better
than to foul their own nests."

We have not only fouled our own nests, we have fouled the nests of every living species on this planet.

We talk about our children as if we have reverence for them, but in truth, what they stand to inherit is a great example of our irreverence not only for our own children, but our children's children, our children's children's children. A common philosophy among some native people is that no decision can be made without considering the impact of that decision seven generations from now.

What is the criteria for making a decision in our culture?

More often than not, the only criteria is how much money do we stand to make?

We talk about the future as if it is some far away place down the road. In actuality, we are thrust into the future every second. The future is upon us.

We tend to think of power as being outside ourselves, but power has always been with the people by virtue of what we choose to support with our finances, who we choose to work for and what we choose to do for money. We could change the health care system in the United States just by refusing to purchase insurance.

If we could have harnessed the energy and participation that is spent on Super Bowl Sunday to protest the Iraq war in February, 2003 - we wouldn't be at war. It is our civic responsibility to be part of the solution.

You don't have to take on every issue, just take on one. First realize that you have the most power to affect change in the community you live in. Start with the problems that face the people in your own communities and find solutions at that level.

For example: change your community from a car culture to a bike culture by establishing bike paths and adding reliable mass transportation such as buses. If this were accomplished, it would result in massive amounts of fuel saved, less pollution, less noise and less death for wildlife populations. Healthcare costs would decrease as a result of physical exercise. Drug costs would dwindle because people would inherently feel better.

If community gardens were established, we could consume only what we grew locally. There again, massive amounts of fuel would be saved because there would be no need to ship food clear around the world or truck it in from outside sources. Healthcare costs would continue to lower because food ripening on the vine and grown locally would be more nutritional. People would know the source of their food and be familiar with the techniques of cultivation.

Relationships with land and other species would be possible by living with and in close proximity to wilderness. A sense of our real purpose in the world would emerge. Once we embrace our responsibility to a particular place, we find it difficult to leave. A life of devotion and love evolves for community and the earth.

Kathy Kelly, Wangari Mathai, Ralph Nader, Aung San Su Kyi, Amy Goodman, Winnona LaDuke, Julia Butterfly Hill; they aren't sitting on a mountaintop praying for a different world, they walk in the world, they belong to the world.

Puma

I hiked along the rim of the gorge wrestling for balance as the wind swept over the mesa, pushing me closer to the edge. Here the earth is split by water spitting up thousands of boulders in protest. The terrain is scattered with toys of the gods, building blocks or marbles the size of a small planet. Stark white bones frozen in the posture of death are strewn across these mammoth brown stones accessible only to large cats.

A pungent odor likened only to urine burned the inside of my nostrils. My eyes widened as I peered between the shadows of rock and earth. I continued to walk, one foot in front of the other. As my adrenaline escalated, I deepened my breath to calm the beat of my racing heart. I stepped and turned, gliding forward, stumbling upon a huge pile of fresh scat. I stood over the steaming pile digesting the serious nature of this warning. I scanned the horizon and then trekked across the mesa far away from the gorge.

Spirit

As water reflects a face
So a man's heart reflects the man.

- Proverbs 27:19

Finally, I want you to consider the Amish. The Amish are a group of Anabaptist Christians who migrated to the United States in the 18th century to avoid religious persecution. They speak a German dialect referred to as Pennsylvania Dutch, and they dress in traditional clothing similar if not the same as the clothes their ancestors wore.

This is a community of people who have for the most part rejected our lifestyle. Their lives are not dictated by the needs of electricity and oil. They live and work close to the land, raise and educate their children, grow their own food, make their own clothes, build their own homes and tend to their spiritual and creative communities. They travel by foot, bicycle or by horse and carriage. They have no police force because their communities are void of crime. They accept no assistance from financial or government institutions. They have no insurance, no social security or retirement funds to draw from.

In October, 2006, an outsider held a group of Amish schoolchildren hostage in their own schoolhouse. Five of those children were shot dead before the gunman took his own life. The Amish community responded to this tragedy by not only forgiving the assailant, but seventy-five members of this community attended the gunman's funeral, and offered monetary and emotional support to the gunman's family. Their vision is not clouded or cluttered by the distractions of electronics or the roar of engines. Their vision is clear, their path is unobstructed, and their hearts are as wide as the sky.

To find God, you must welcome everything.

- Rabindranath Tagore

Do our hearts reflect love and forgiveness or revenge and violence? Do our hearts reflect integrity and honor or deceit and betrayal? How do we live with less ego, less greed, less aggression and less fear?

Perhaps, we begin by facing our prejudices - be they sexual, gender, religion, skin color, cultural differences or dislike for specific plant and animal species. We have to attend to the world as it was created and not force our own vision of what the creation should look like or be.

Some native people believe that the earth has a memory of wherever you walk. What will the earth's memory be of us?

Gandhi walked across the continent of India to mobilize a nation to strike for its independence from Great Britain. He did it without the Internet, television or telephones. The problems facing us today require all of our hearts and minds. Time, however, is not on our side.

If we truly want our children as well as the children of all species to have a future, we need to do everything possible to reduce our own impact on this planet. We don't need leaders. We don't need to organize or join groups. All we need to do is change our own lives.

If we could only see the world as it is, we might awaken our indigenous hearts and begin to cultivate our own innate wisdom. Once we accept the cycle of life and death, live within the confines of nature, listen rather then speak, we could change the course of our evolution. The less we have equals a war free world, a healthier planet and the freedom to pursue the life we dream of living.

Eagle

The glare of the sun fabricates mirages, illusions crafted from light. I rubbed tears of the wind from my eyes and waited to see what remained when the light shifted. Nothing.

I turned to look over my right shoulder - and from behind me, soaring two hundred feet over the gorge, Eagle joined me. As he hovered an arm's length from where I stood, I considered reaching out to him. So close. He dropped to the lower depths of the canyon skirting the crest of water rippling towards the sea.

Peace

Man has accepted conflict
as an innate part of daily existence
because he has accepted competition, jealousy,
greed, acquisitiveness and aggression
as a natural way of life.

- Krishnamurti

February 15, 2003, was the largest international day of protest that the world has ever seen. It was the last significant protest before the United States invaded Iraq. I was invited to speak in Santa Fe at the largest protest New Mexico had ever seen. In closing, I would like to share with you what I expressed that day.

∂❦

In my yoga practice, I move from warrior one into warrior two into reverse warrior. My yoga teacher tells me that these postures are good for developing endurance, to cultivate inner strength in order to face the tough times that lay before us. My teacher's favorite posture is dying warrior. The body is twisted into a vulnerable position where the liver and kidneys are squeezed as you teeter on one knee. The weight of the body is placed in the upper shoulders, the eyes are gazing at the heavens, arms are splayed in surrender, and the breath is labored. I have tremendous difficulty with this posture because I have a great resistance to dying. As I lie in this awkward pose, struggling to give way, the words of my friend Harry come to mind.

Harry was a Buddhist monk for some twenty years in Nepal. I sought him out when I began to plan a trip to India. I was extremely frightened about becoming ill in India; I had many questions concerning vaccinations and medications I might need. He informed me that he never had any vaccinations and as a result, he had contracted everything; malaria, typhoid fever, amoeba dysentery, cholera and hepatitis. He said,

"These are the gifts of India."

I sat across from him in absolute terror.

"The blessing of illness brings you face to face with who you really are. You come to understand what needs to die away in you, so that something else might be awakened."

So I'm in this yoga posture called dying warrior, and with each inhale I confront the despair and grief of this moment. With each exhale I relinquish my struggle.

What is dying in me?

What is dying in us?

What is dying in America?

And what is waiting to be born?

In music, I am the melody.

- The Bhagavad Gita

Enlightenment

www.democracynow.org - National and international news program that can be found on some public radio stations or listened to online.

www.nativeamericatalking.com - Radio program out of Albuquerque, New Mexico, that focuses on issues related to native people.

www.phoenixcommotion.com -Dan Phillips builds homes for the working poor out of salvaged and recycled materials.

BOOKS

Woody Allen, *Side Effects*

Maude Barlow, *Blue Covenant: The Global Water Crisis and the Coming Battle for the Right to Water*

Becky Bee, *The Cob Builders Handbook*

Wendell Berry, *The Art of the Commonplace*: *The Agrarian Essays of Wendell Berry*

Rachel Carson, *Silent Spring*

Pablo Casals, *Joys and Sorrows; Reflections*

Caroline W. Casey, *Making the Gods Work for You*

Pema Chödron, *When Things Fall Apart*
The Places That Scare You

Offerings

Kino Denzer, *Build Your Own Earth Oven*

Ianto Evans, Micheal G. Smith, Linda Smiley, *The Hand-Sculpted House*

Danielle and Olivier Föllmi, *Wisdom*

Massanobu Fukuoka, *The One-Straw Revolution*

Corbin Harney, *The Way It Is: One Water One Air One Mother Earth*

Linda Hogan, *Mean Spirit*
Solar Storms
Power

Ivan Illich, *Deschooling Society*
Energy and Equity

Derrick Jensen, *A Language Older Than Words*
Culture of Make Believe

Joseph Kennedy, Micheal G. Smith, Catherine Wanek, *The Art of Natural Building*

J. Krishnamurti, *Total Freedom*

Satish Kumar, *Path Without Destination*

Winnona Laduke, *All Our Relations*

Barry Lopez, *Arctic Dreams*

Edward Mazria, *The Passive Solar Energy Book*

Ralph Nader, *The Seventeen Traditions*

Anita Roddick, *Business as Unusual*

Theodore Roszak, *Voice of the Earth*

Arundhati Roy, *The Cost of Living*

John Schaeffer, *Solar Living Source Book*

E. F. Schumacher, *Small is Beautiful*

Vandana Shiva, *Staying Alive*

Malidoma Patrice Somé, *Of Water and the Spirit Ritual*

Athena and Bill Steen, *The Beauty of Straw Bale Houses Small Straw Bale*

Rabindranath Tagore, *Sadhana: The Realisation of Life*

Swami Vivekananda, *The Complete Works of Swami Vivekananda*

Howard Zinn, *A People's History of the United States 1492 - Present*

FILM

An Unreasonable Man - Documentary on the life and contributions of Ralph Nader.

Being Caribou - Documentary of the Porcupine Caribou herd as they migrate towards their calving grounds in Northern Canada. Produced by newlyweds who took a six-month honeymoon to film this journey.

Body of War - Documentary about soldier Tomas Young returning home from the war in Iraq paralyzed from the chest down.

The End of Suburbia: Oil Depletion and the Collapse of the American Dream - Documentary

Flow: For the Love of Water - Documentary on the scarcity of water, the world's most crucial resource.

Homeland: Four Portraits of Native Action - Documentary on the environmental issues facing four native communities in Alaska, New Mexico, Wyoming and Maine.

Spring, Summer, Fall, Winter . . .and then Spring - Korean film about the stages of man.

The Take - Documentary about the economic collapse of Argentina and the people's comeback.

Who Killed the Electric Car? - Documentary about the beginning and demise of the electric battery car.

Notes

1. Lao Tzu - Chinese philosopher.

2. Theodore Roszak - American professor, writer and social thinker. Used with permission.

3. Mahatma Gandhi - Indian lawyer who fought for independence through non-violence and civil disobedience.

4. Pablo Casals - Spanish cellist and conductor.

5. Woody Allen - "The Speech to the Graduates," *Side Effects* © Ballantine Books, 1980. Used with permission.

6. Freidrich Nietzsche - "Maxims and Arrows," *Twilight of the Idols*, 1889.

7. Buddha - Indian sage whose major teaching was *The Lotus Sutra*.

8. Swami Vivekananda - *The Complete Works of Swami Vivekananda Vol. IX, Calcutta* © Advaita Ashrama, 1989. Used with permission.

9. E.F. Schumacher - "Buddhist Economics," *Small is Beautiful* © Hartley and Marks Publishers, 1973. Used with permission.

10. Phillip Berrigan - Founder of Jonah House. Peace activist, priest, husband and father. Used with permission.

11. Mother Teresa's words © Missionaries of Charity Sisters c/o Mother Teresa Center, 2008. Used with permission.

12. Wendell Berry from *The Art of the Commonplace: The Agrarian Essays of Wendell Berry* © Wendell Berry, 2003. Reprinted by permission of the publisher.

13. Betsy Smith - Aquatic biologist and artist. Used with permission.

14. "Proverbs" - *Book of the Bible*, King James version. Teachings on how to live a wise and ethical life.

15. Rabindranath Tagore – *Sadhana* © Editions Albin Michel, Paris - 1940, 1971, 1996. Used with permission.

16. Jiddu Krishnamurti - *Freedom From the Known* © Krishnamurti Foundation Trust Limited, UK , 1989. Used with permission.
     www.kfoundation.org
     www.kfa.org

17. *The Bhagavad Gita* - Indian text concerned with acquiring spiritual liberation and union through yoga.

Acknowledgments

We may come into this world alone and depart from it alone, but while we are here, it is only through the grace of others that we ever accomplish anything. I humbly thank -

Sarah Morgan for her limitless generosity.

All of my students, friends and family whose own lives have been nothing less than a source of inspiration and great encouragement:

In Texas - Lyric Muckleroy, Debbie Bush, Kim Kennamer, Amy Sanford, Connie Calhoun, Deda Divine, Kyle Childress, Kerry Lemon, Denise McDonald, Betsy Smith, Marilyn Eanes, Matt Salas, Buckley MacInerney, the congregation of Austin Heights Baptist Church, Rohini and Kiran Patel, the devotees of Sai Shivam Temple, Elizabeth Cerri Morgan, the family clanships of Morgan and Muckleroy.

In New Mexico - Robin Collier, Victoria Seale, Fred and Daryl Black, Suzanne Weiss, Mike Tilley, Beryl Schwartz, Dirk Sullivan, Cynthia Holmire, Alita Randolph, Stephen Bradley, Ella-Kari Loftfield, Raj Mooty, Emily Kienzle, Mary Mercier, Pat Di Vasto, Susie Schwartz.

Beyond and abroad - Suzanne Bullard, Garfield Morgan, Ellen Shade, Marianne Watson, Diane Hill, Ruth Wegahaupt, Paymon Kayhani, Chris and Charlie Powell, Marcia Schwartz.

My greatest teachers on loyalty, forgiveness, and unconditional love - Fox, a feral tomcat, Sass, a red stallion, and Taffy, a toy poodle.